A VISUAL DIARY

A Selection of
Caricature Drawings
October 2, 2020 - January 20, 2021

BRENDA LOUIE

Library of Congress Data on file. ISBN 978-1-953978-30-1

...for Kurt

How this book was created.

*Art can blow us out of our pigeonhole. In deafness it may
shout or scream, in blindness it may arrest our attention, in
numbness it may shake up our mind. If we don't sense
anything at all and take everything for granted, art can kick
us in the ass, give a conscience and make us aware.*
–Erik Pevernagie

Drawing helps fuel my imagination and find clarity for my inner
thoughts. Creating a series of drawings that intensely channels my
emotions allows me to look back at what I witnessed and how I felt
during that period.

A Visual Diary was my first attempt presenting in a caricature format.
These works were derived from a series of rapid sketches created daily
during the dreadful time of the U.S. presidential election period, from
October 2, 2020 to January 20, 2021, and were refined in the following
months.

I want these drawings to serve as a means of documenting my
personal, horrific, raw fears and anxieties during an unprecedented
global virus attack of COVID-19 and the resulting Lockdown while
I stayed home alone watching the unsettled political and social
chaos unfold from a TV set between the end of the election year that
transitioned into the beginning of a new presidency on January 20,
2021.

The selected drawings in this book were taken from a body of more than
200 drawings and sketches. Most of these drawings were made with simple
materials like black and red pens on 9 x 12 inch regular drawing paper.

Brenda Louie
2024

Four Years of Screaming
2016 - 2020

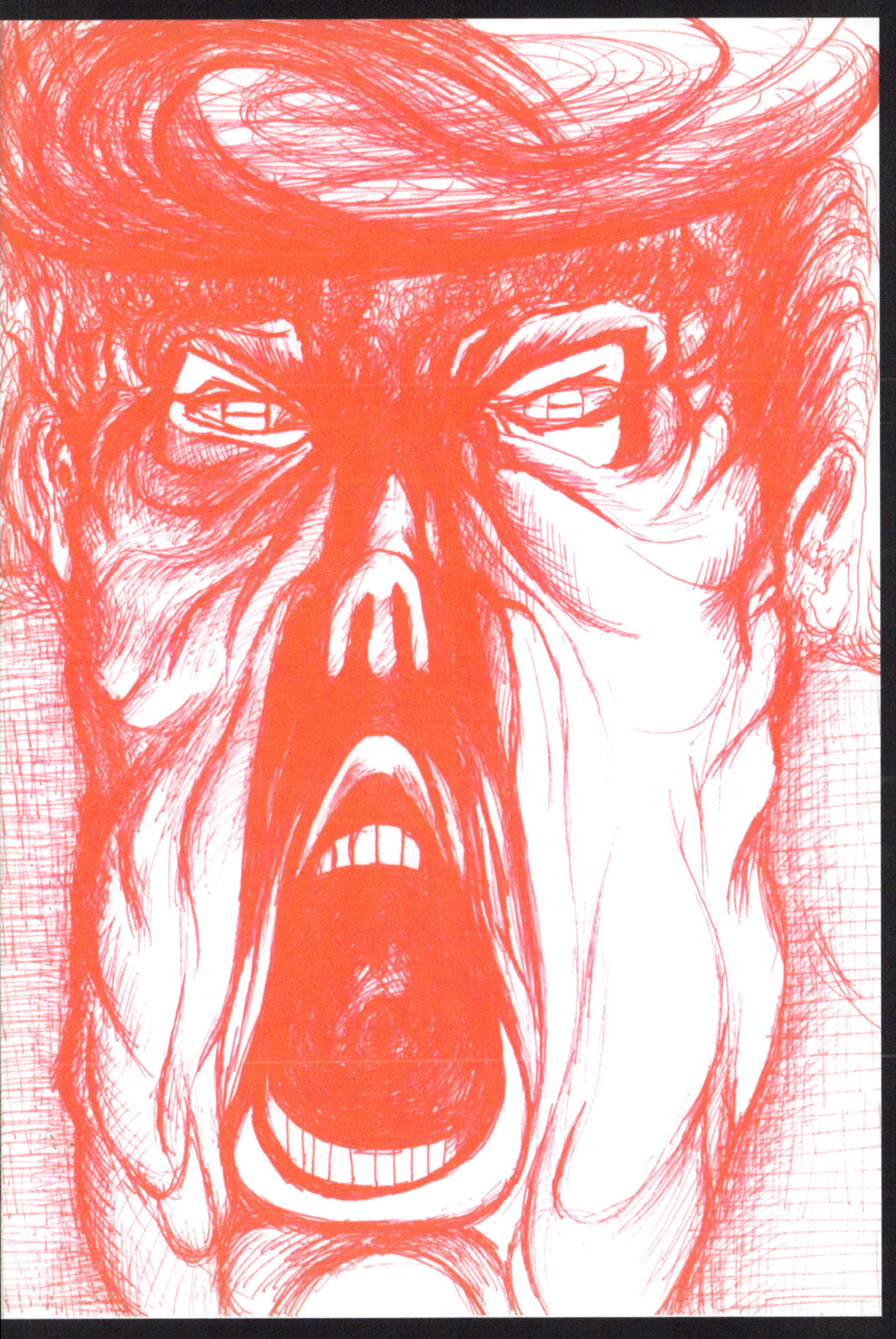

"The self-righteous scream judgments against others to hide the noise of skeletons dancing in their own closets."

John Mark Green

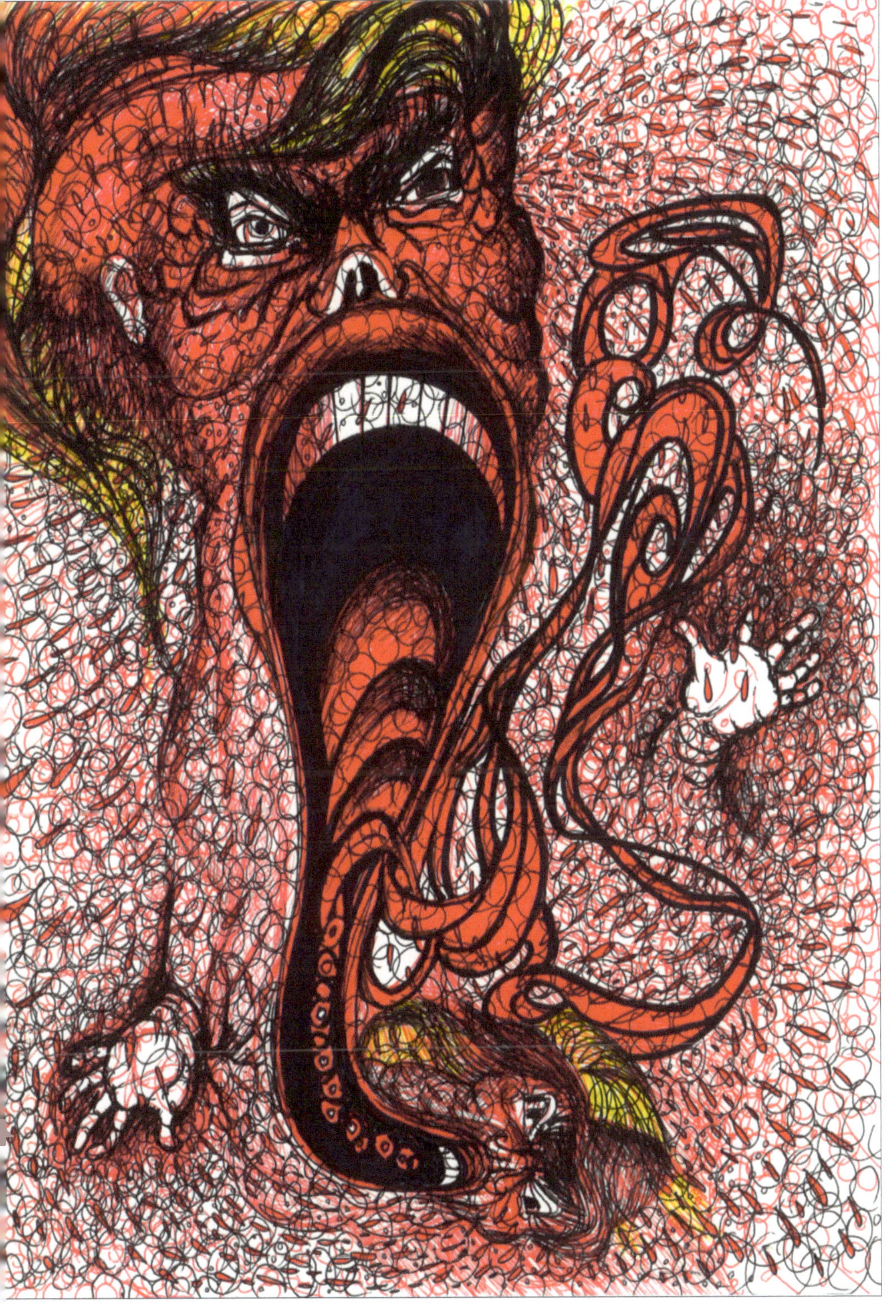

Superspread
in the White House
October 2020

This unprecedented pandemic, COVID-19, killed millions globally,
including 250,000 deaths in the U.S. in 2020, while many of those
deaths could have been prevented if the government had followed the
scientific recommendations to implement appropriate social practices.

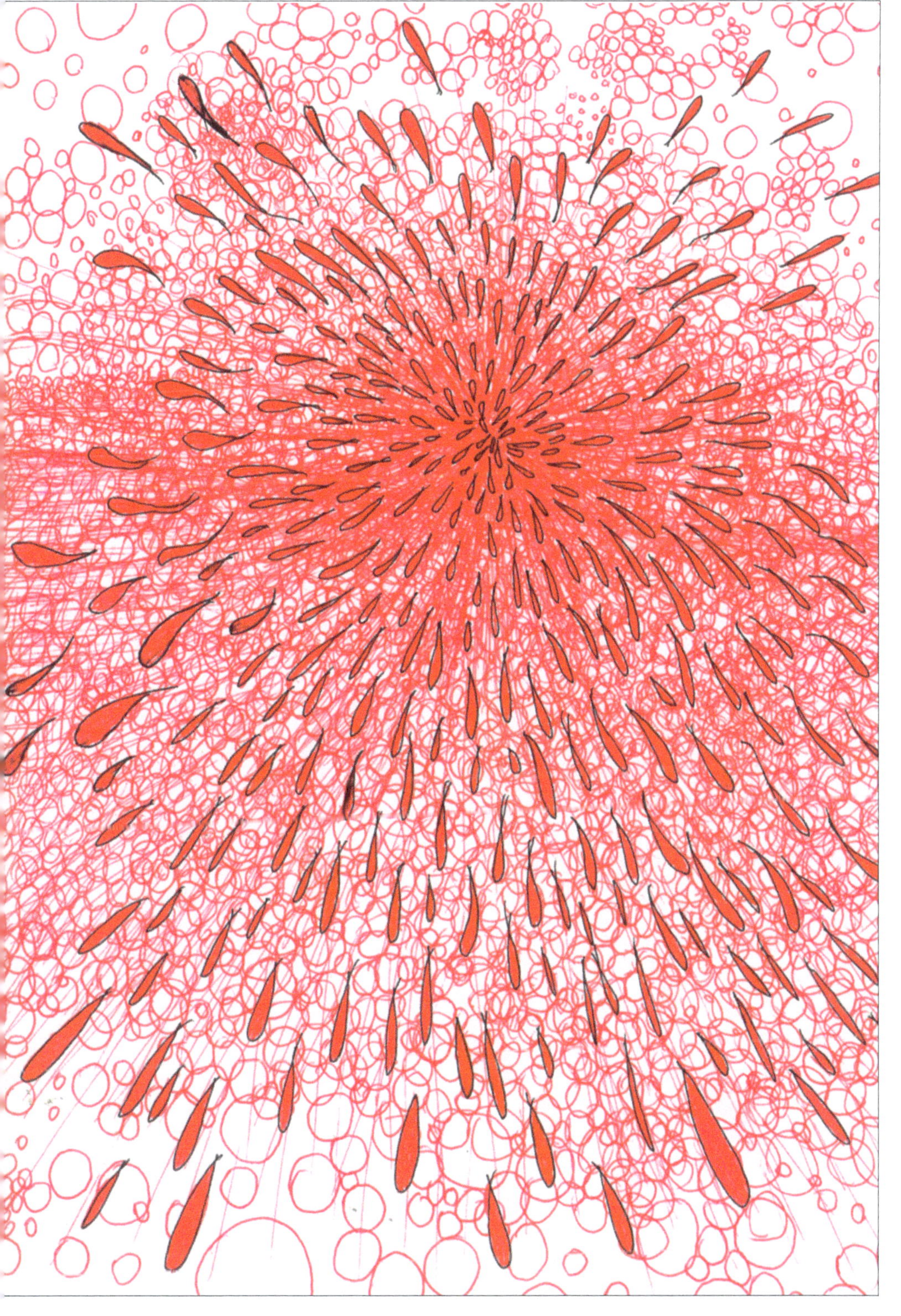

Trump's positive COVID-19 test
threw the country into fresh upheaval.

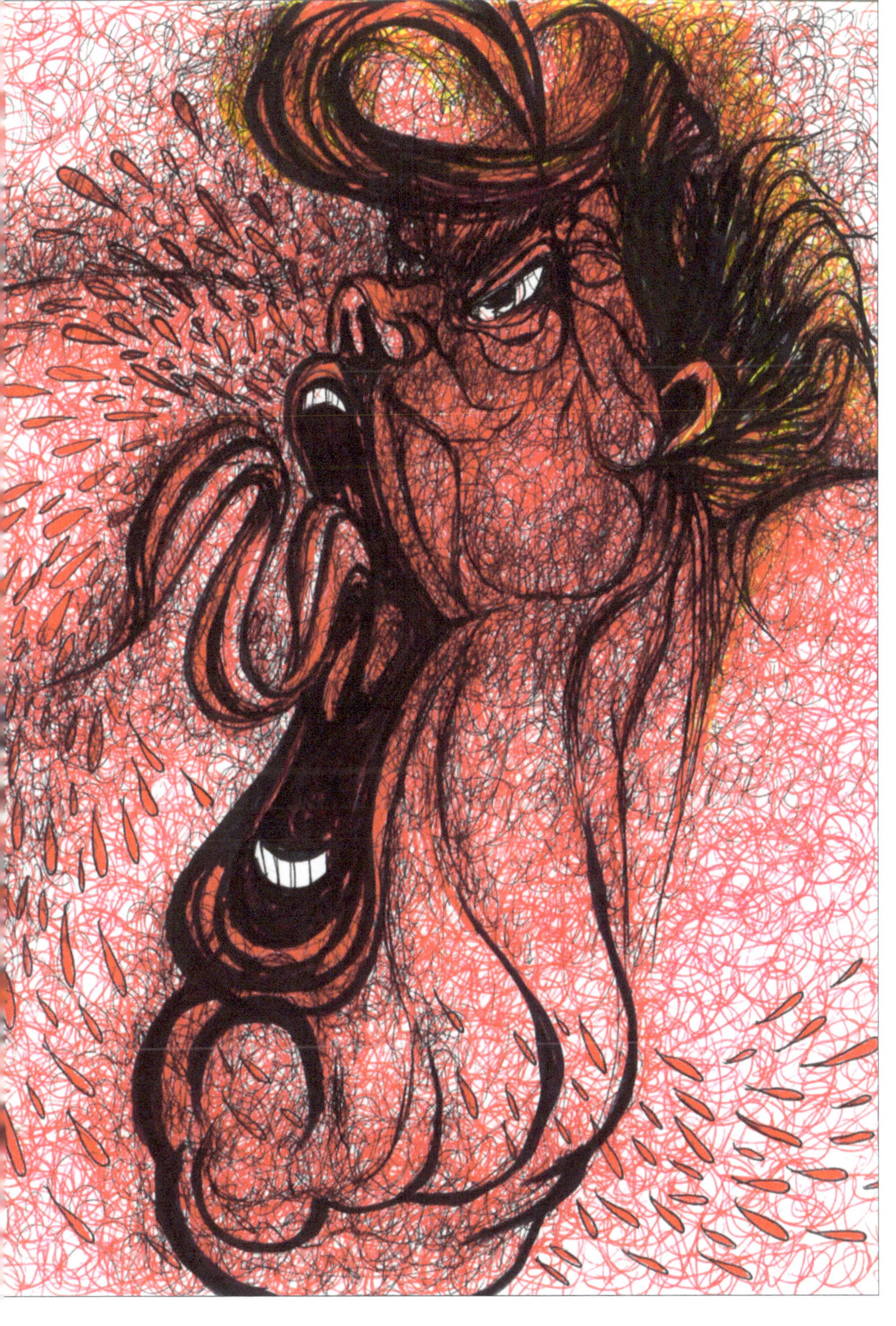

President Donald Trump announced Friday, October 2, 2020 that
he and the First Lady had tested positive for Coronavirus, a
stunning development that threatened the security of the nation.

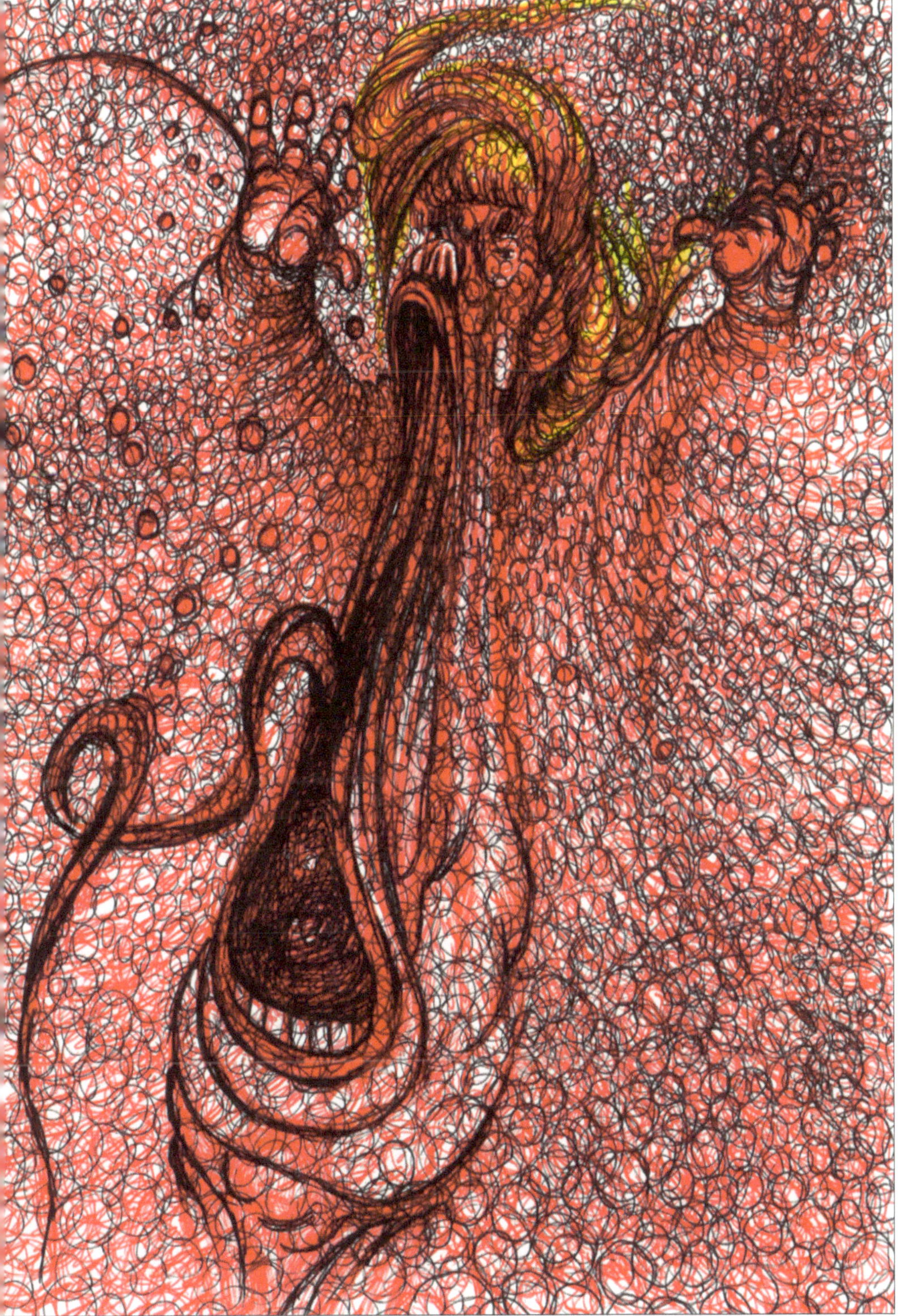

Later that day, Trump was transferred to Walter Reed
National Military Medical Center.

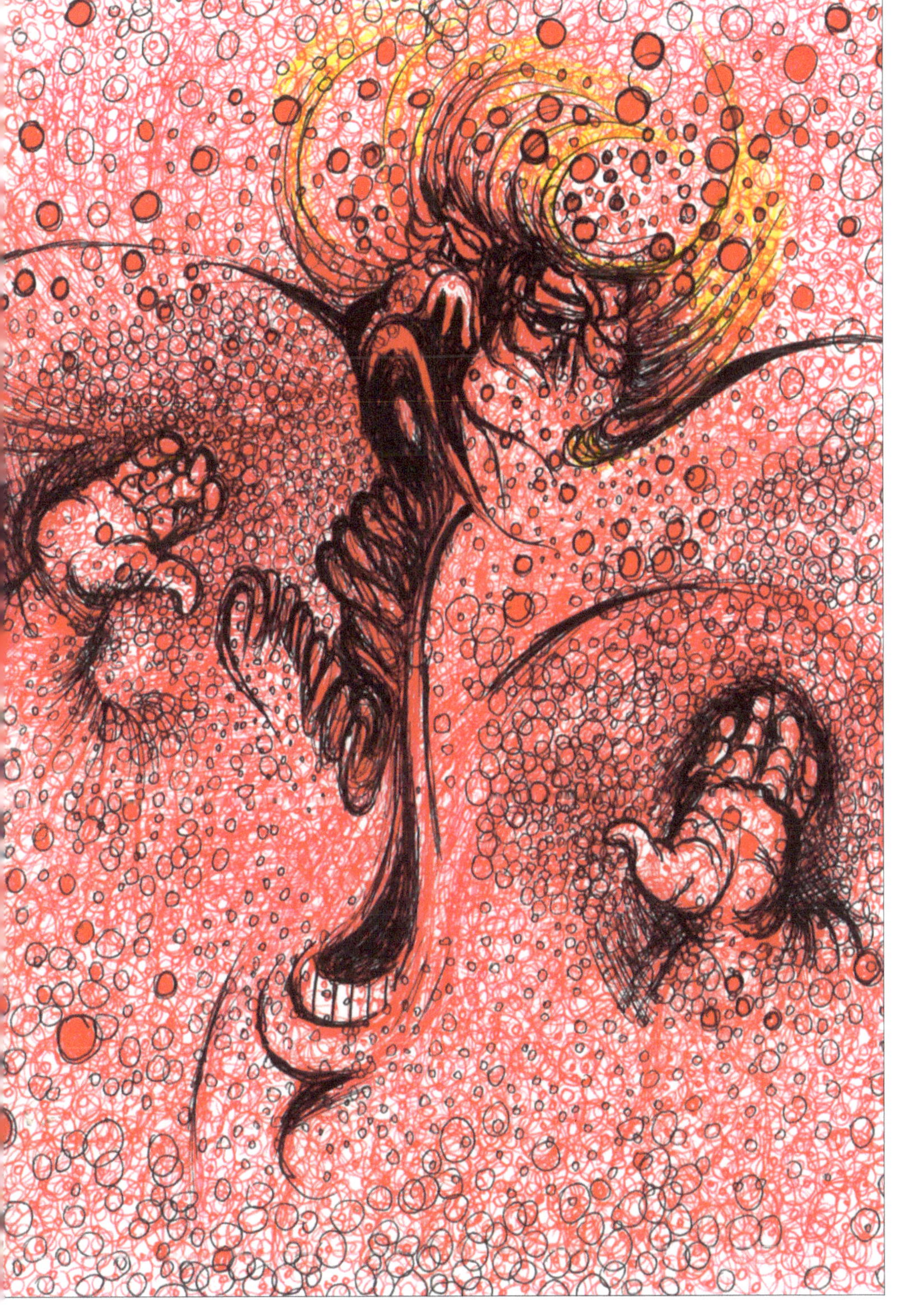

More than a dozen members of Trump's circle also tested positive
including press secretary Kayleigh McEnany, senior advisor
Stephen Miller, campaign manager Bill Stepien and assistant to
the president Nicholas Luna.

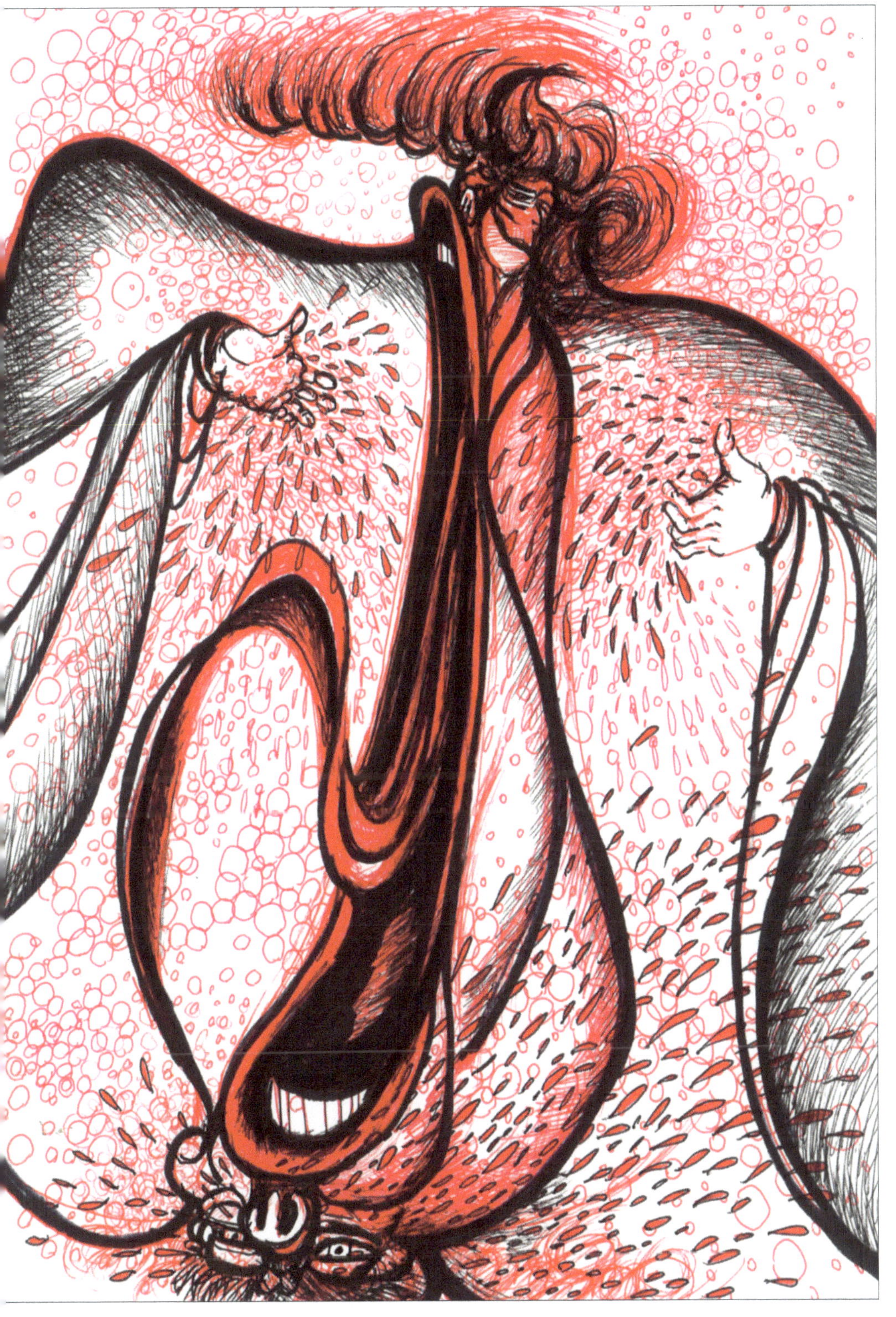

FEAR

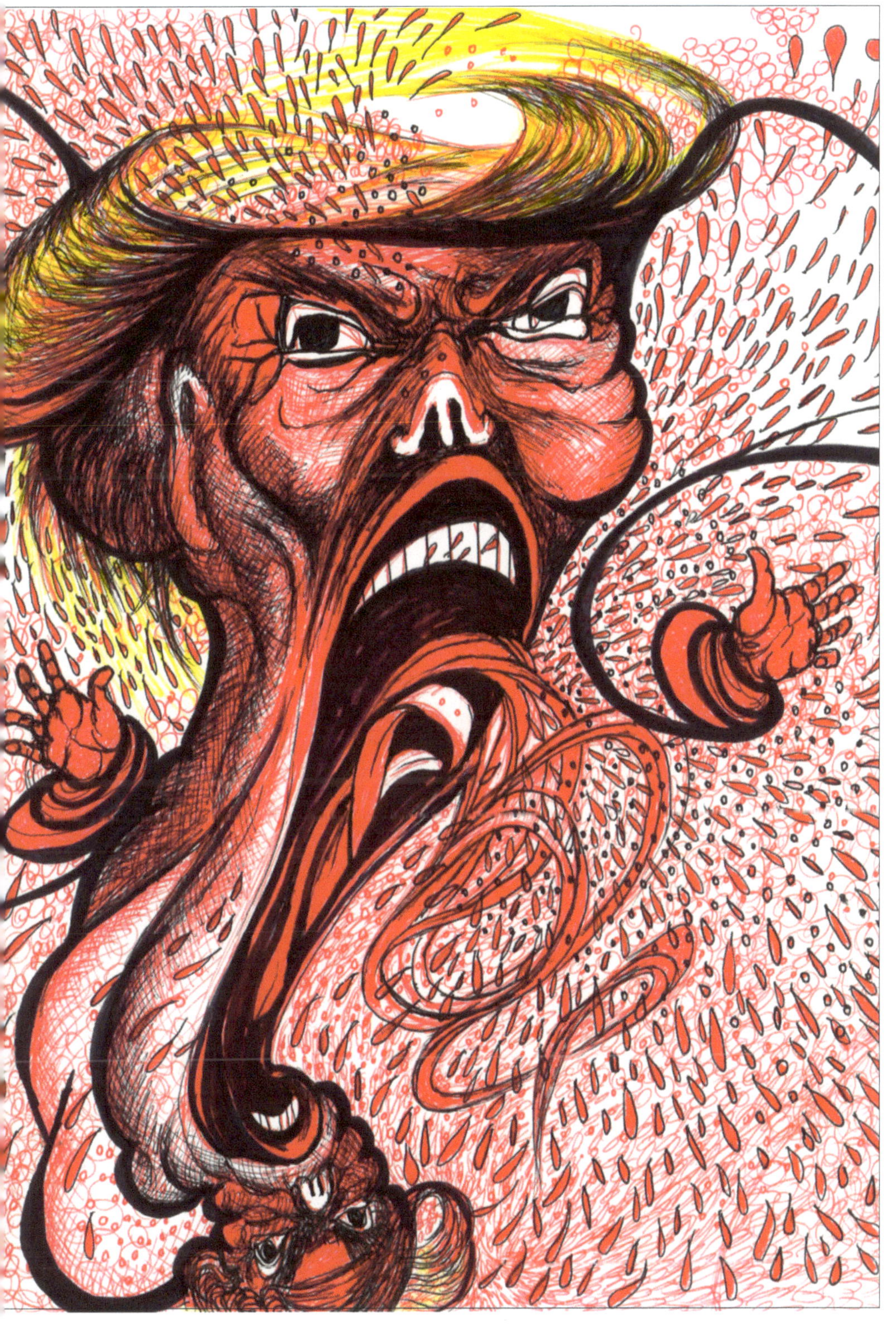

FEAR

FEAR

FEAR

FEAR

FEAR

FEAR FEAR

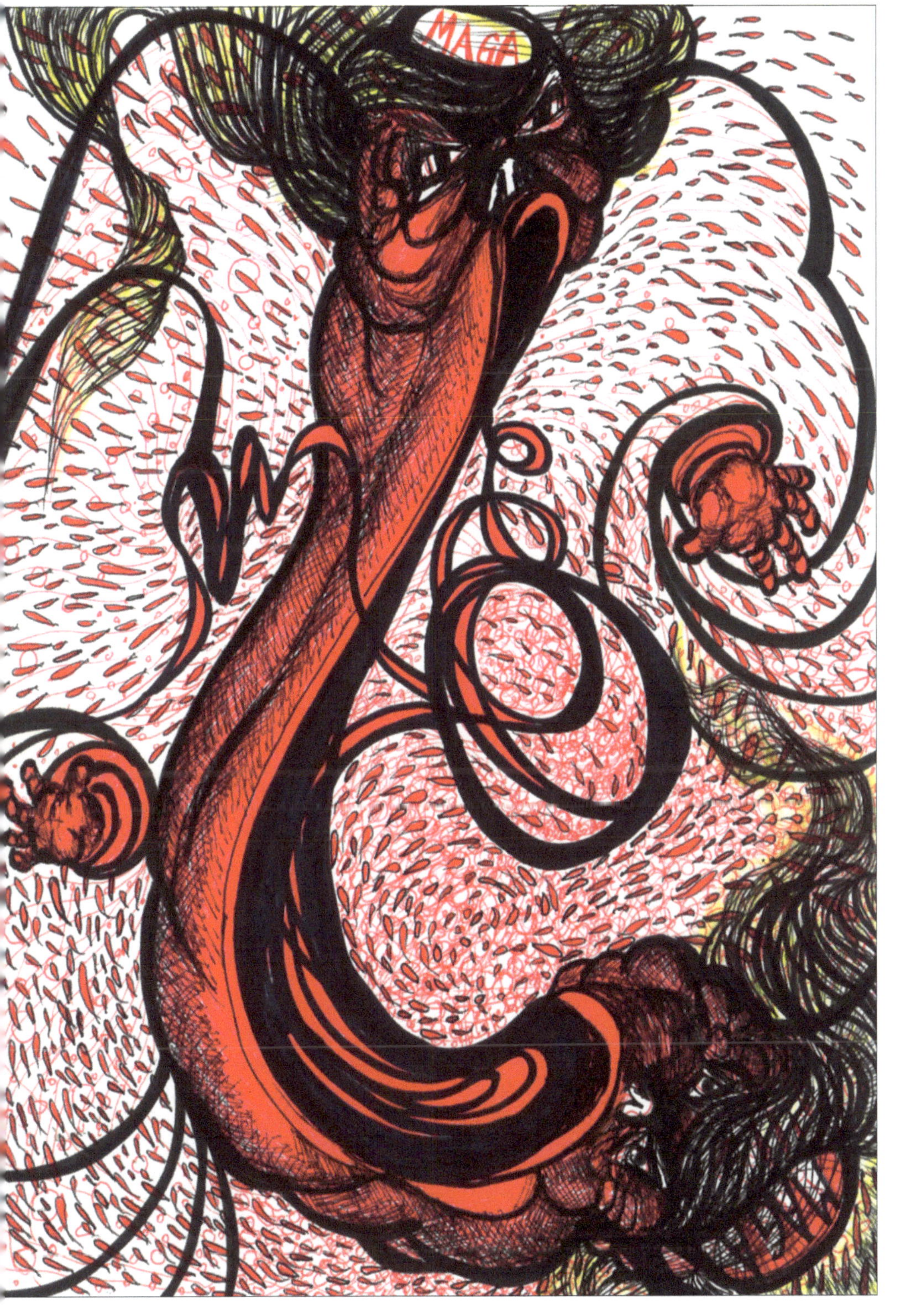
MAGA

*"The power of the people
is stronger than the people in power."*

Bono

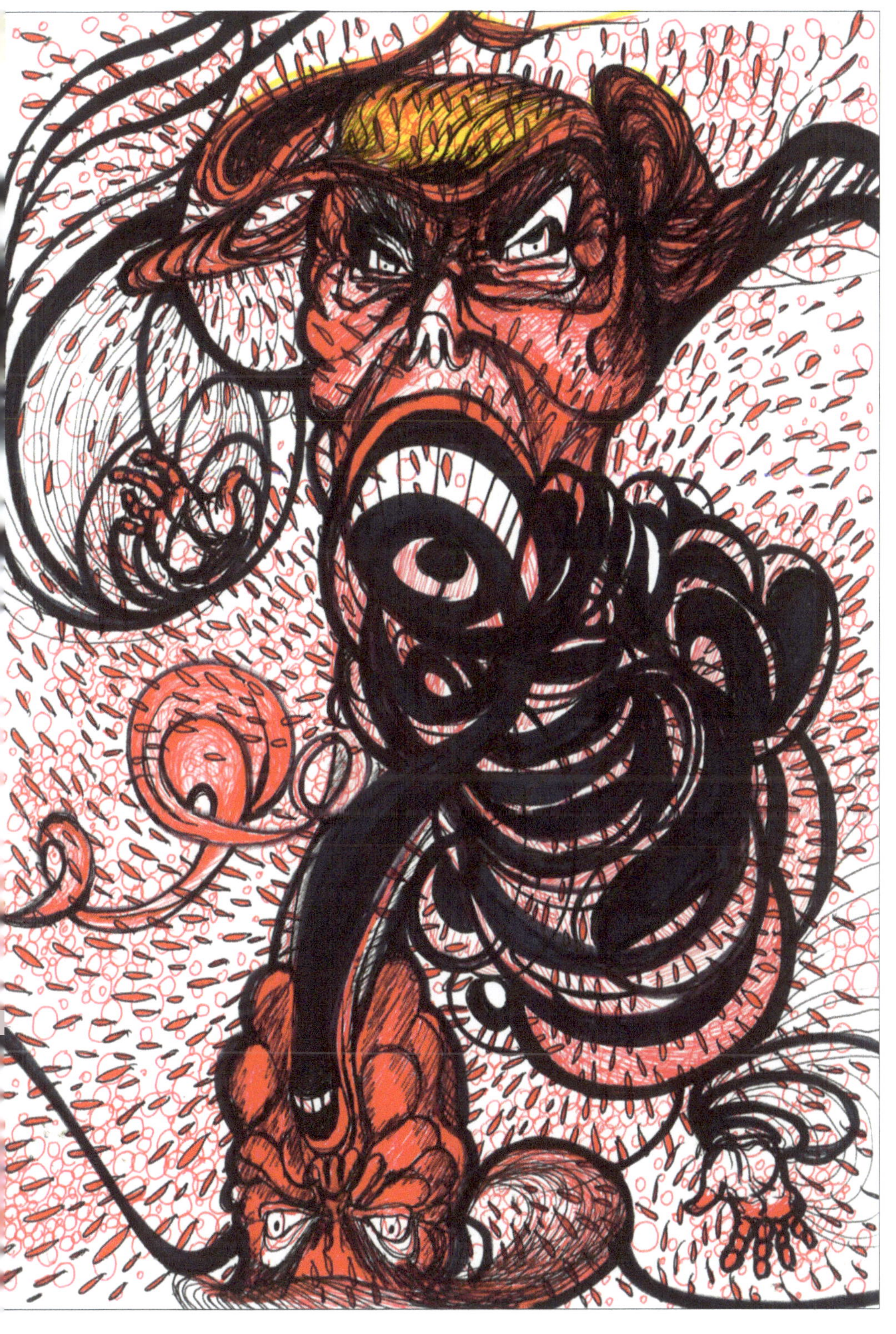

*"Two things are infinite: the universe and human stupidity;
and I'm not sure about the universe."*

Albert Einstein

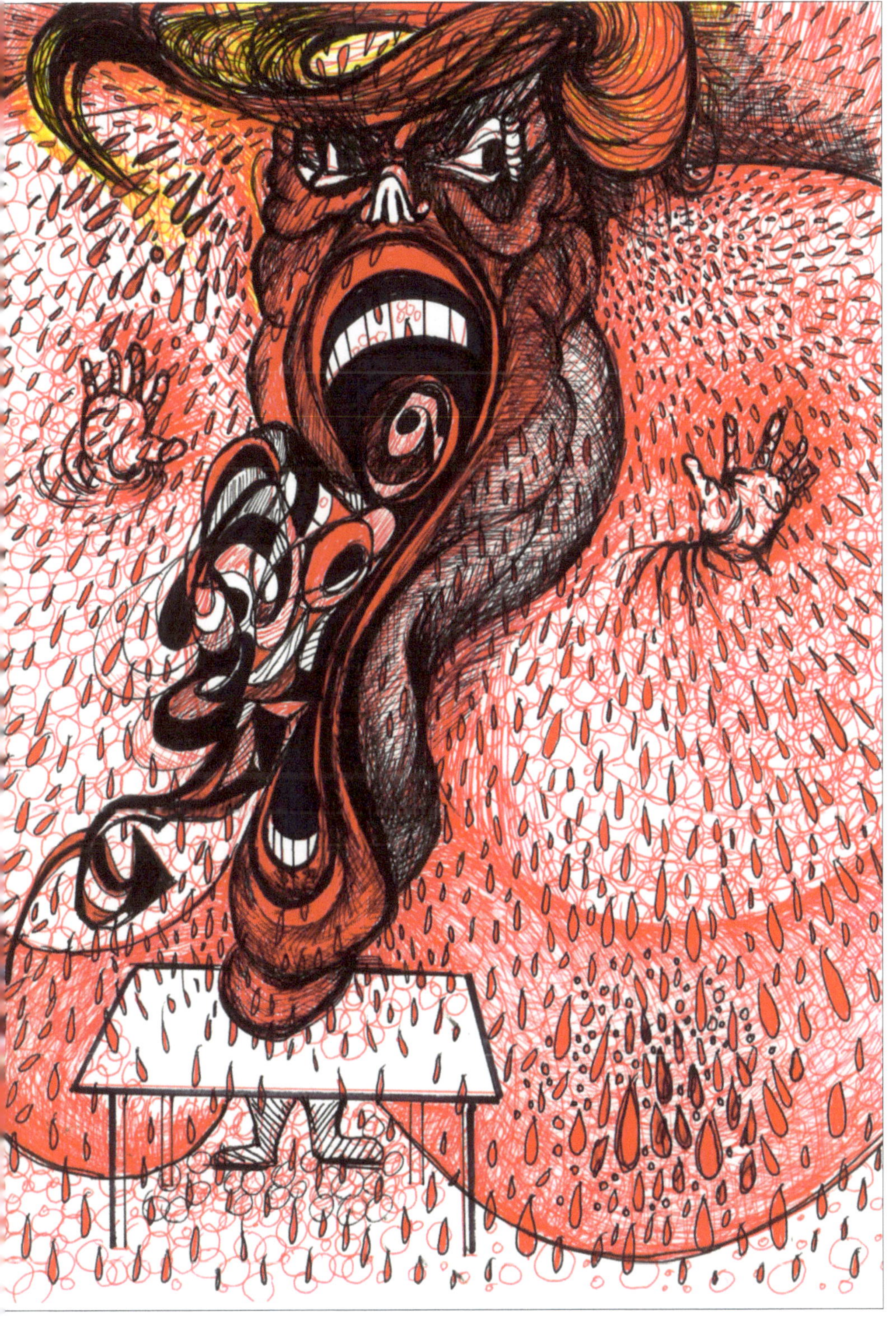

"Save America!"
January 6, 2021

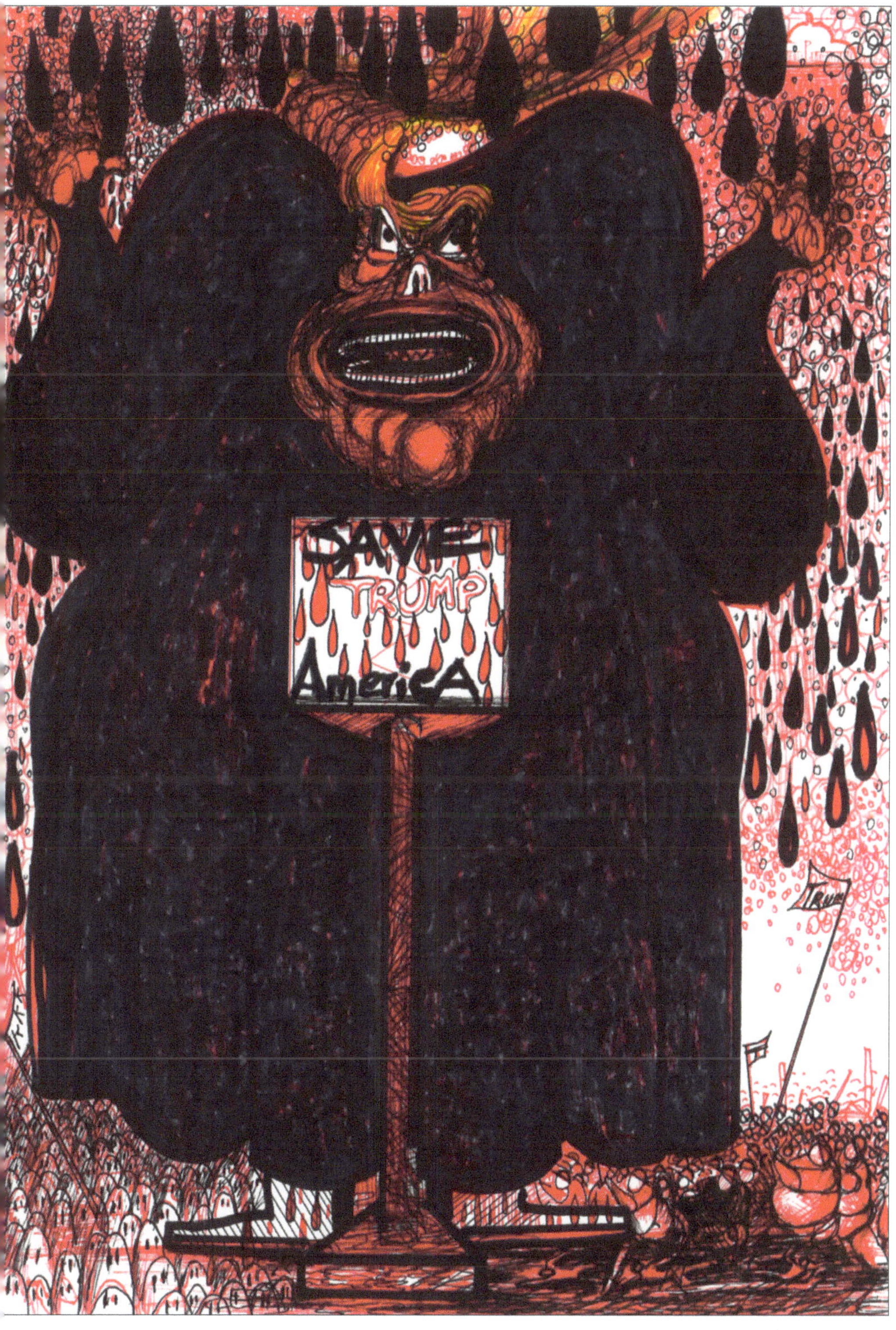
SAVE
TRUMP
America

At 1:10 p.m. on January 6,
President Trump concluded
his speech at the Ellipse.

I remembered vividly the riot erupting following
Trump's morning speech near the Capitol.

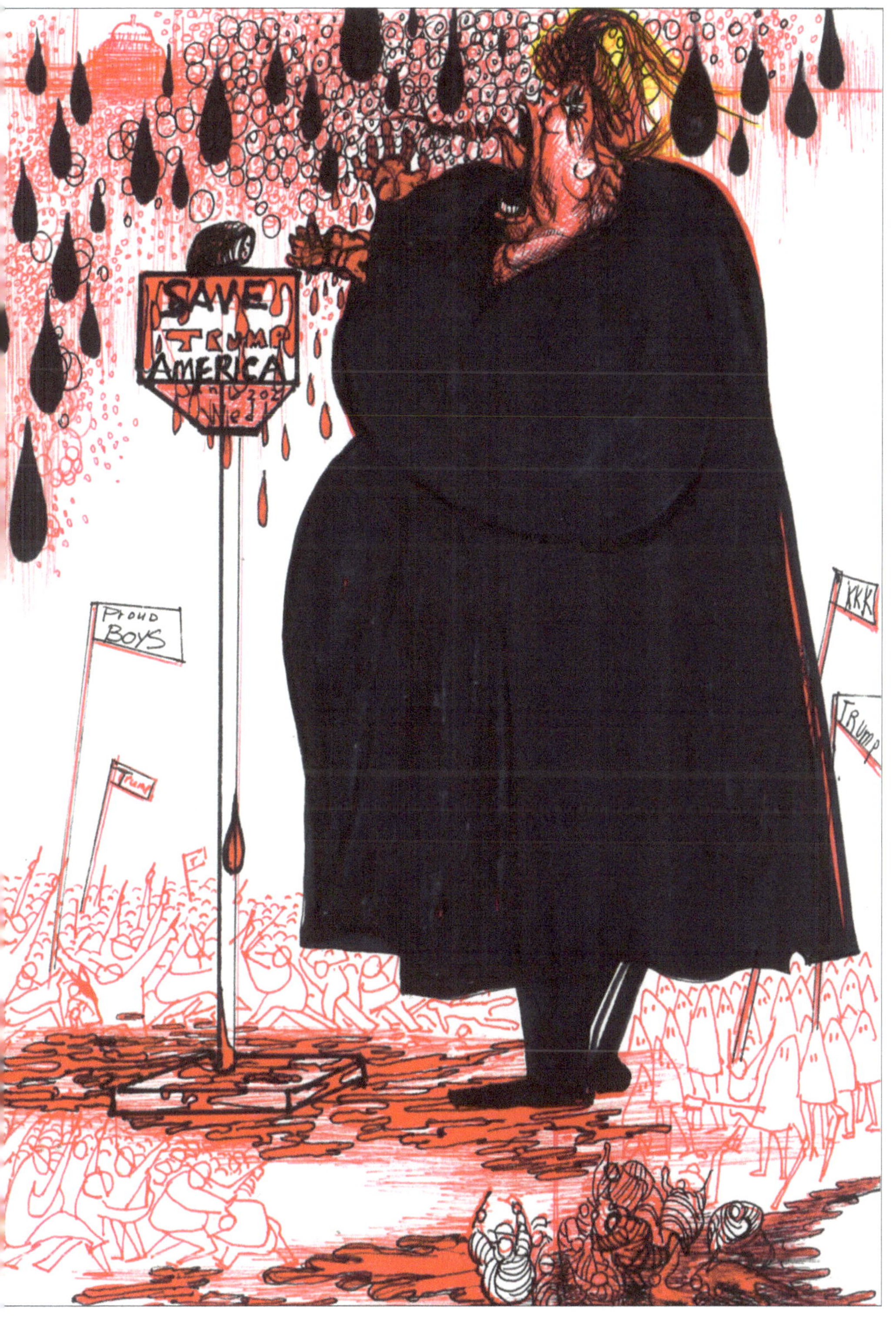

SAVE
TRUMP
AMERICA
PROUD
BOYS
Trump
KKK
TRUMP

By that time, the attack on the U.S. Capitol had already begun. But it
was about to get much worse. The President told thousands of people
in attendance to march down Pennsylvania Avenue to the Capitol.

He told them to "fight like hell"
because if they didn't, they were
"not going to have a country anymore."

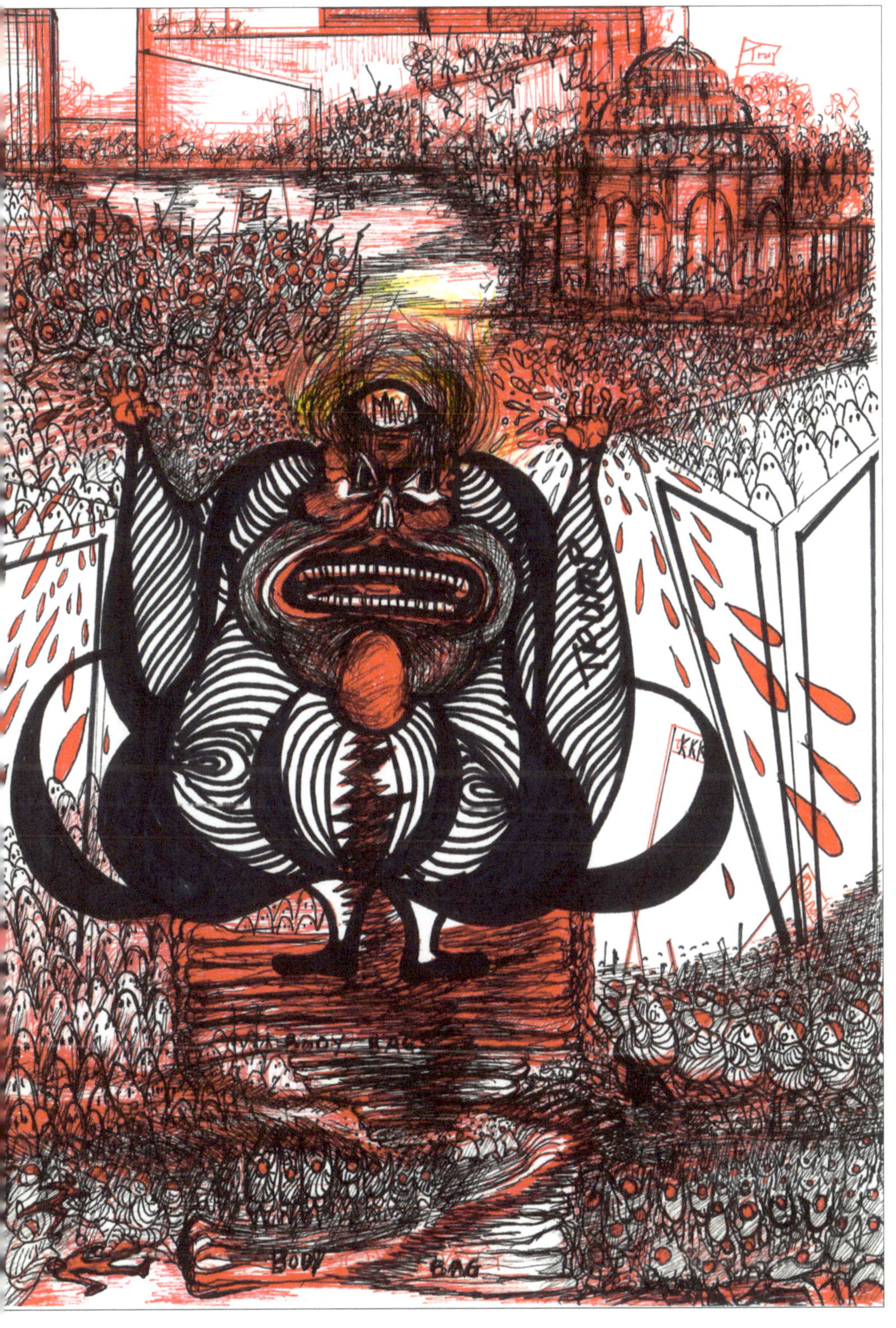

MAGA
TRU
KKK
BODY BAG

By 1:21 p.m., President Trump was informed that
the Capitol was under attack.

He could have interceded immediately.

But the President chose not to do so.
It was not until 4:17 p.m. that President Trump finally tweeted a
video in which he told the rioters to go home.

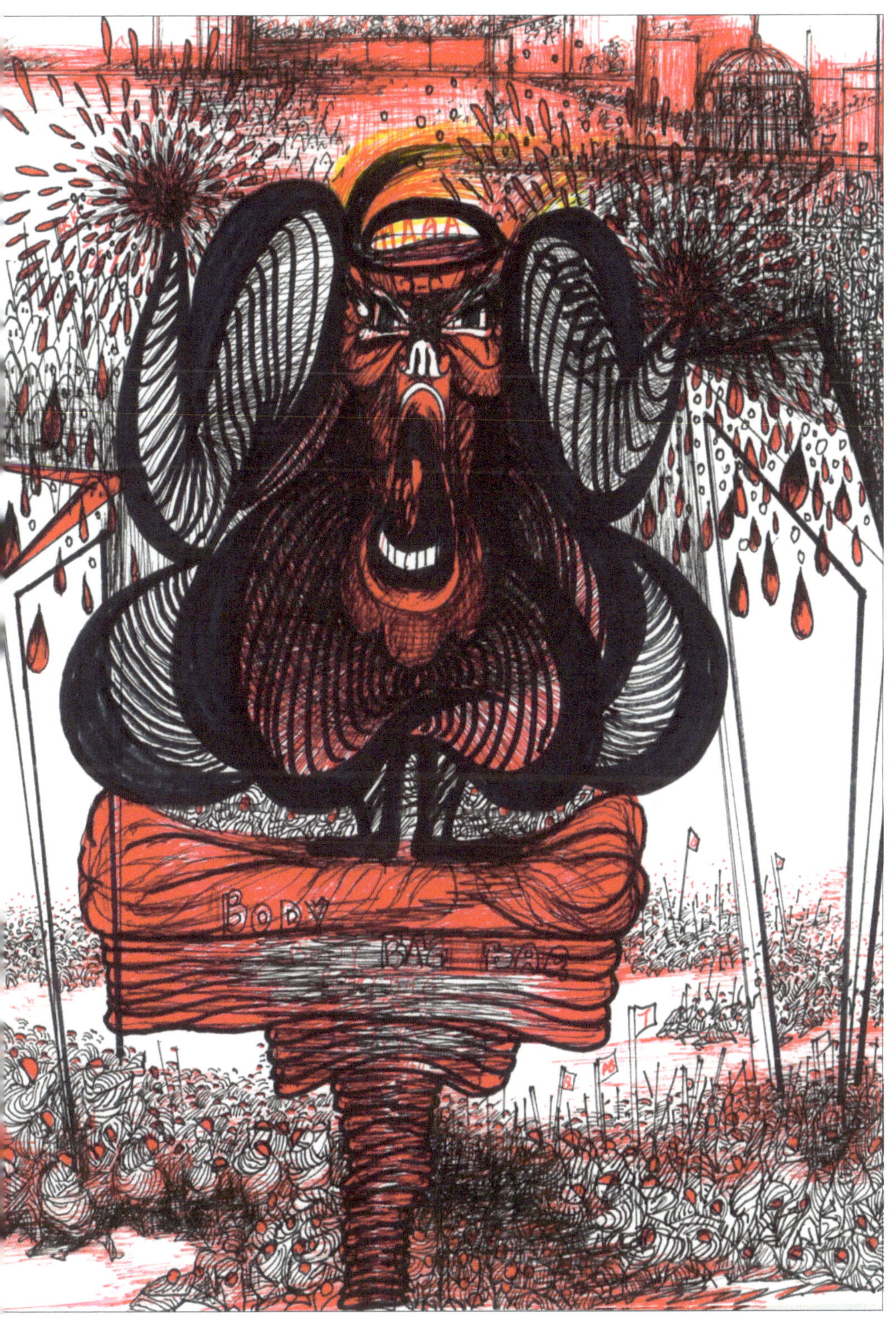

BODY BAG BAR

"Misinformation is the new weapon of mass distraction. Opportunists are using it to start a war or to gain support. Most people are killed, violated, arrested, assaulted, accused, hated, cancelled, or sanctioned because of misinformation. Choose to validate everything you read or hear so that you don't become a victim of misinformation."

De Philosopher Dj Kyos

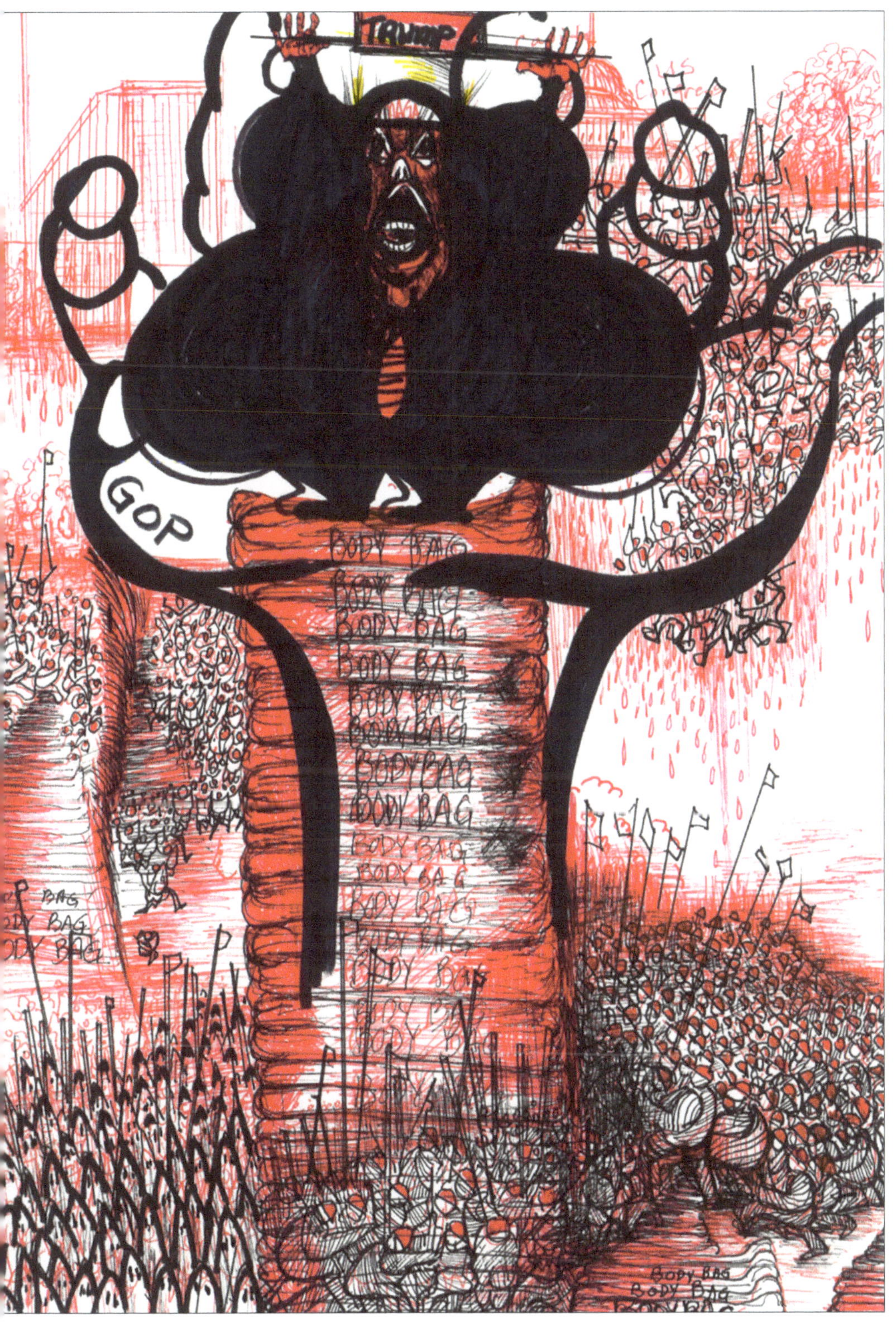
TRUMP
GOP
BODY BAG
BODY BAG
BODY BAG
BODY BAG
BODY BAG
BODY BAG
BODY BAG
BODY BAG
BODY BAG
BODY BAG
BODY BAG
BODY BAG
BODY BAG
BODY BAG
BODY BAG
BODY BAG
BODY BAG
BODY BAG

That, in fact, is how the American right had come to deal with reality:
just throw so much misinformation out there that the public becomes
unable to discern fact from fiction—at which point right-wing
authoritarians will naturally embrace their lying propaganda.

Ex-Trump advisor Stephen Bannon calls it "flooding the zone with shit,"
creating so much uncertainty with a barrage of disinformation that
many people default to the word of their preferred authority figures.

David Neiwert
The Age of Insurrection:
The Radical Right's Assault on American Democracy

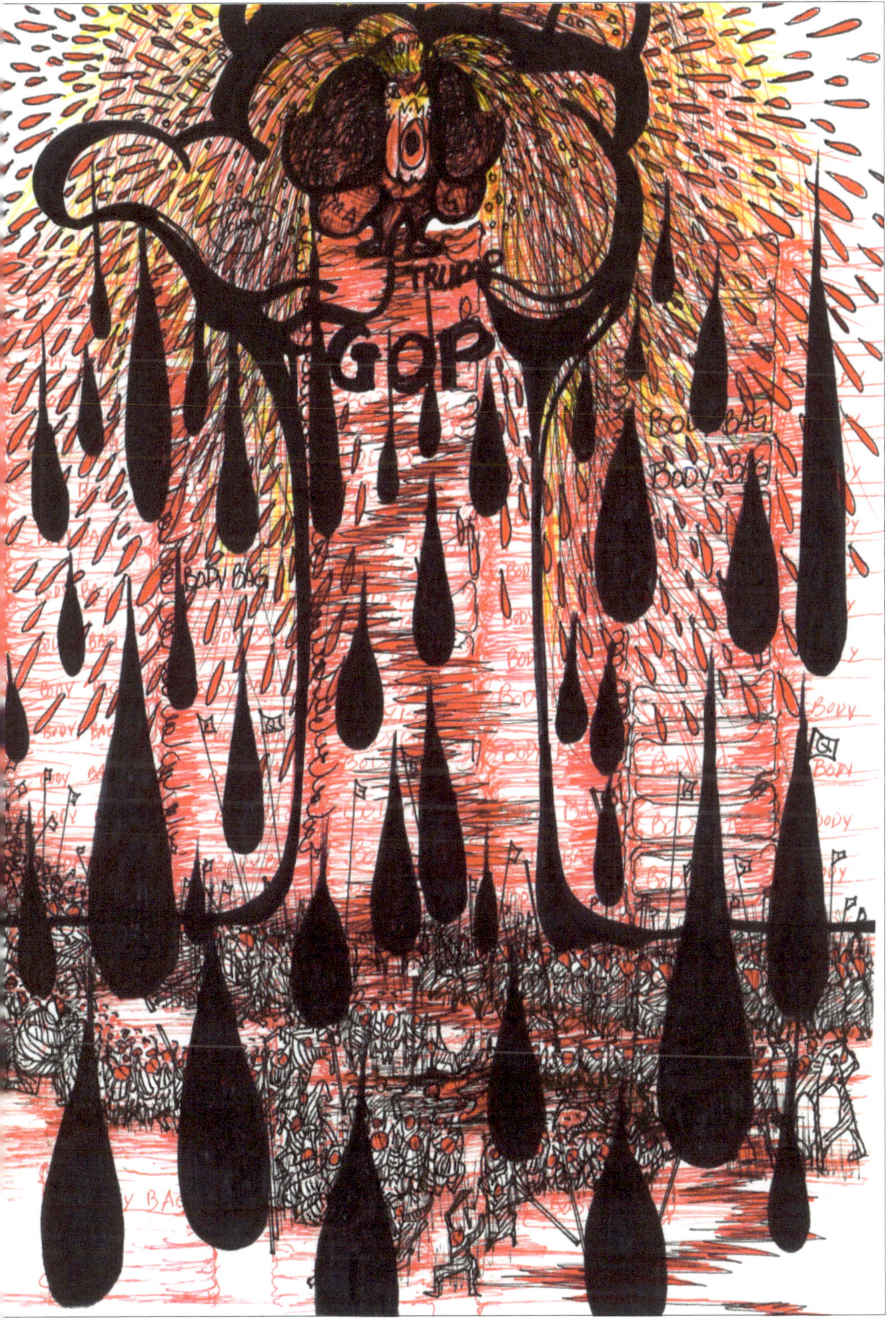

TRUMP
GOP
BODY BAG
BODY BAG
BODY BAG
BODY
BODY
BODY
BODY

"Men use thought only as authority for their injustice and employ speech only to conceal their thoughts."

Voltaire

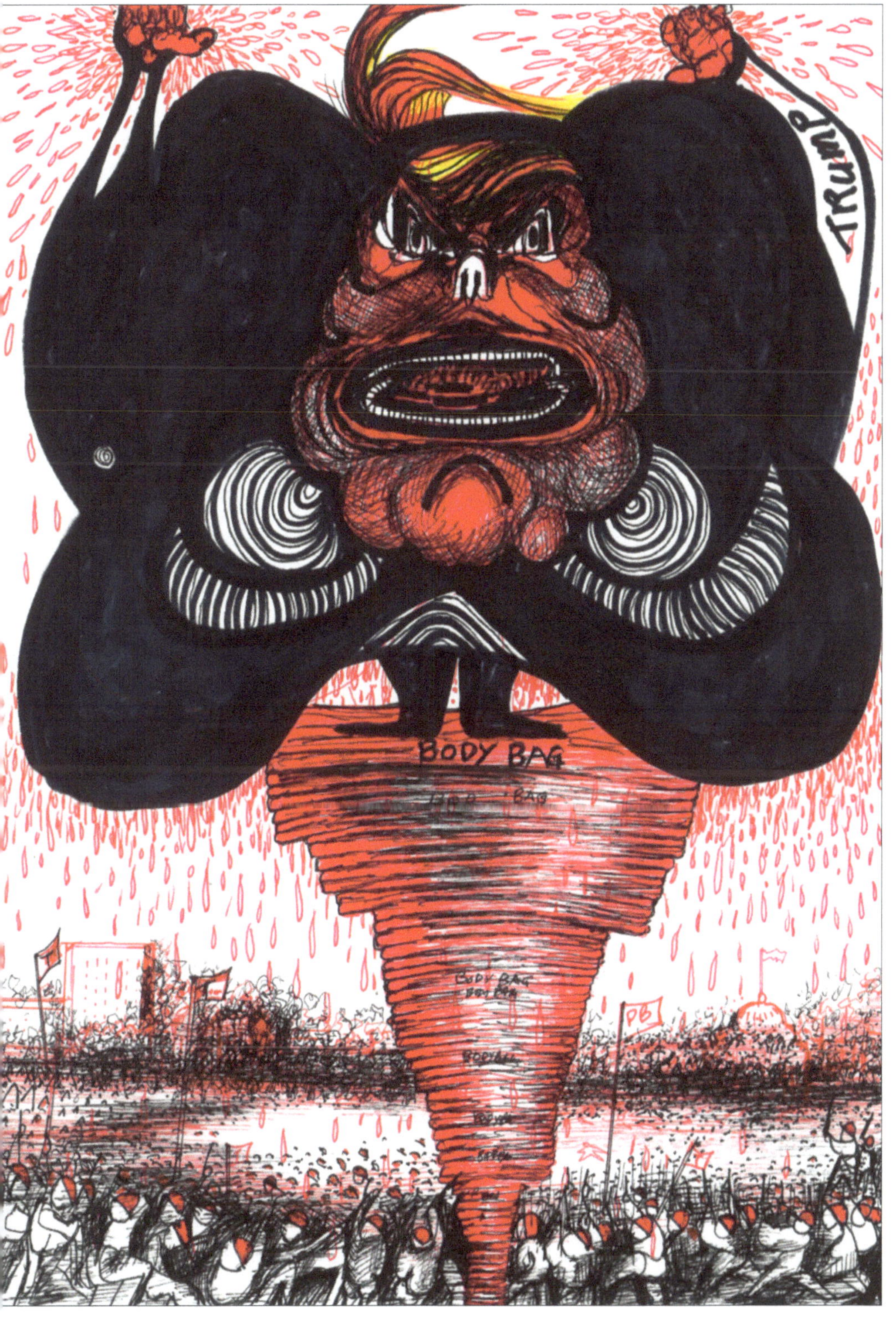

TRUMP
BODY BAG
BODY BAG
BODY BAG
BODY BAG
BODY BAG
BB

"Stand Back!"
"Stand By!"

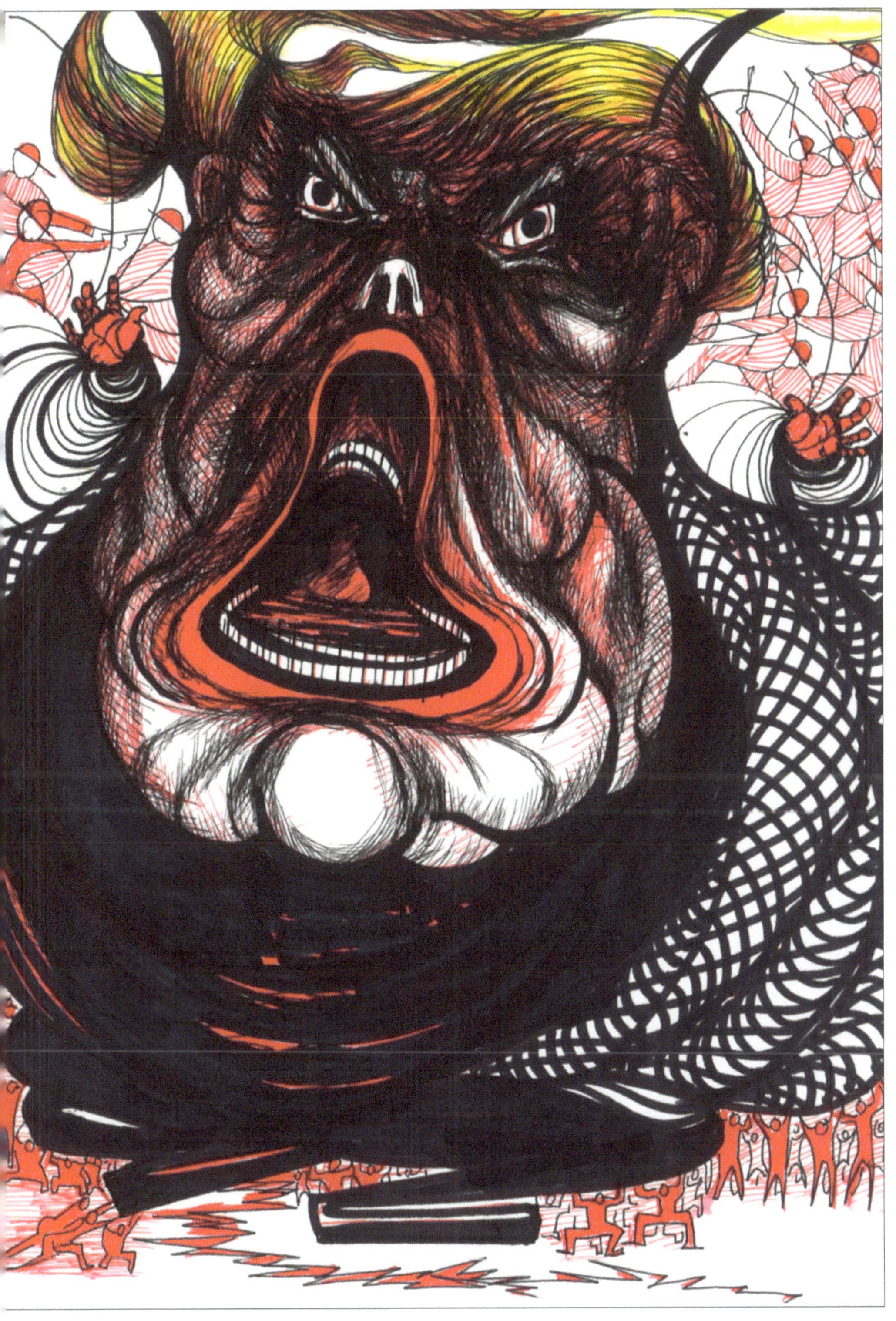

Debate moderator Chris Wallace asked Trump if he was willing
to condemn white supremacists and militia groups, and Biden
interjected to mention the Proud Boys in particular.

Trump said:
"Proud Boys, stand back and stand by."

CNN Politics Facts First

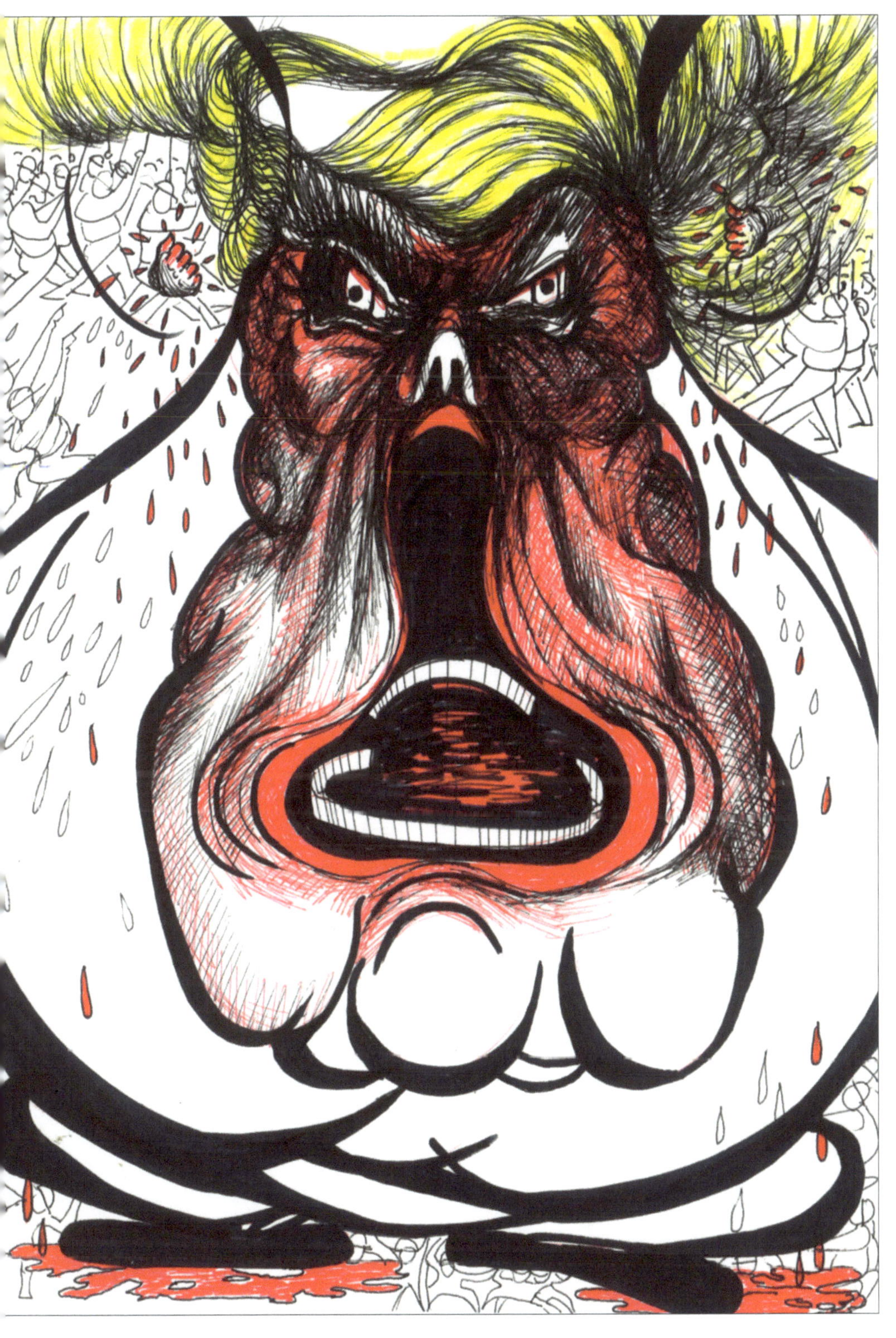

"Social justice cannot be attained by violence. Violence kills what it intends to create."

Pope John Paul II

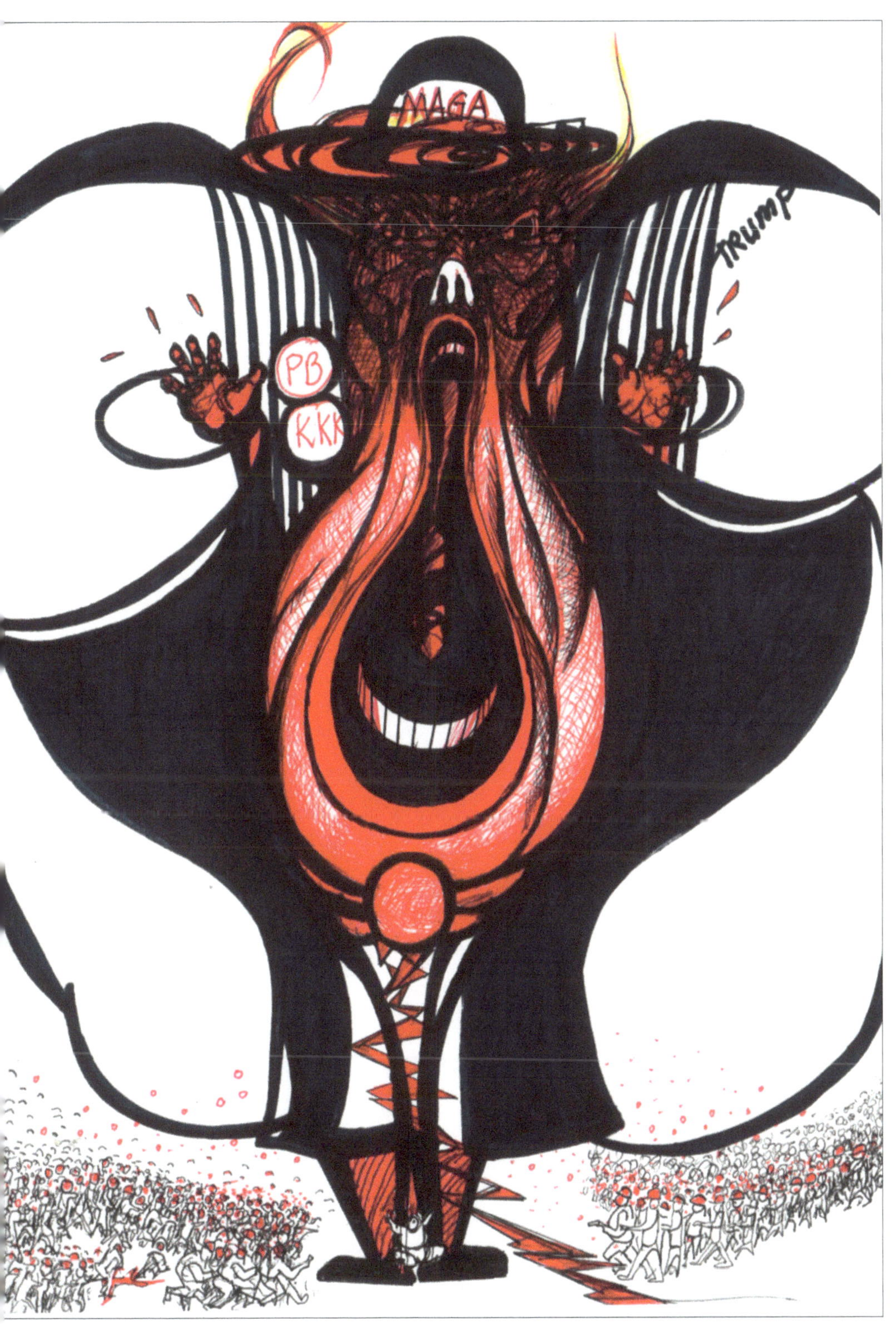

MAGA
TRUMP
PB
KKK

"Those who can make you believe absurdities can make you commit atrocities."

Voltaire

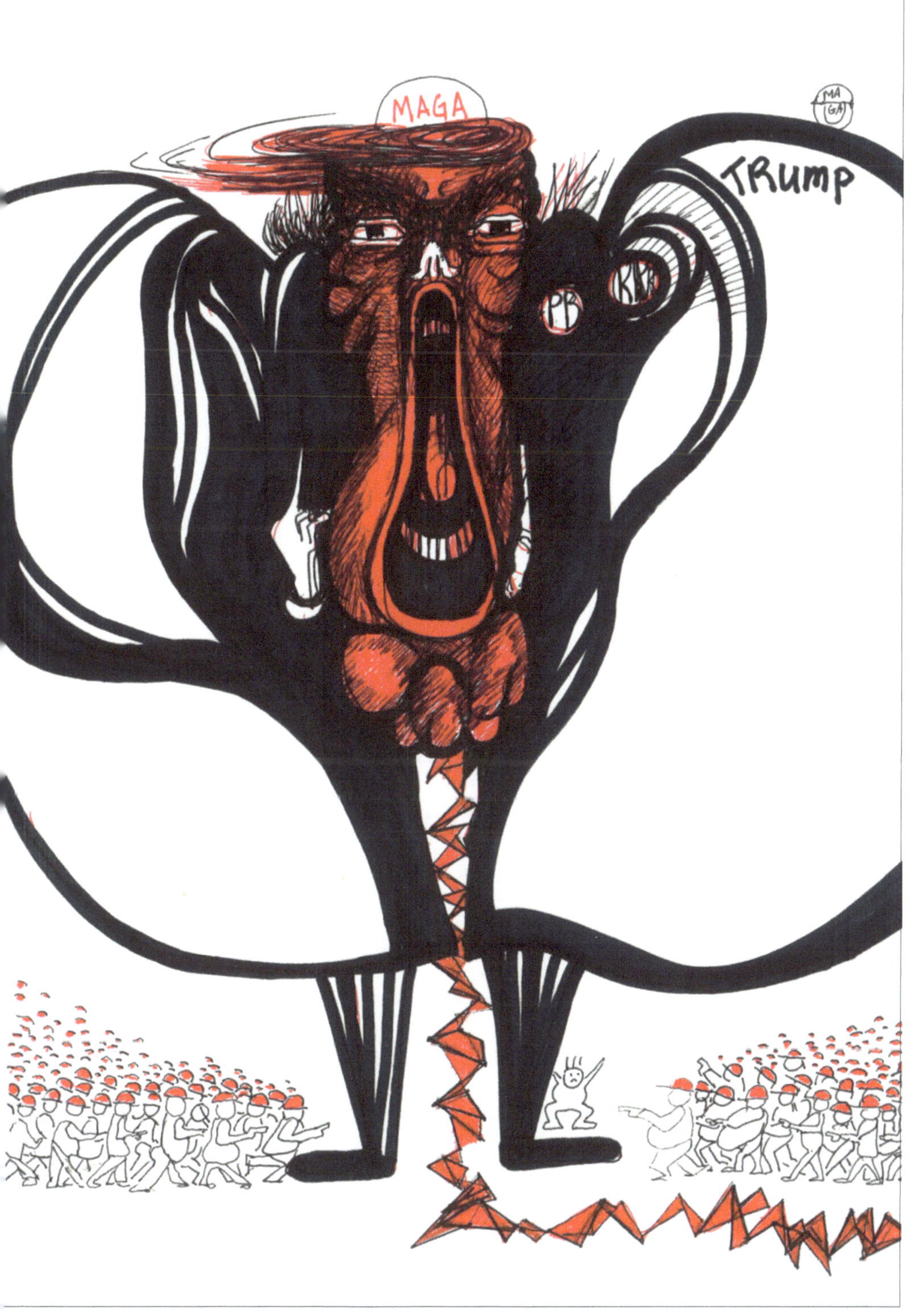

MAGA
MA GA
TRUMP
PB
KKK

"Bag Man"

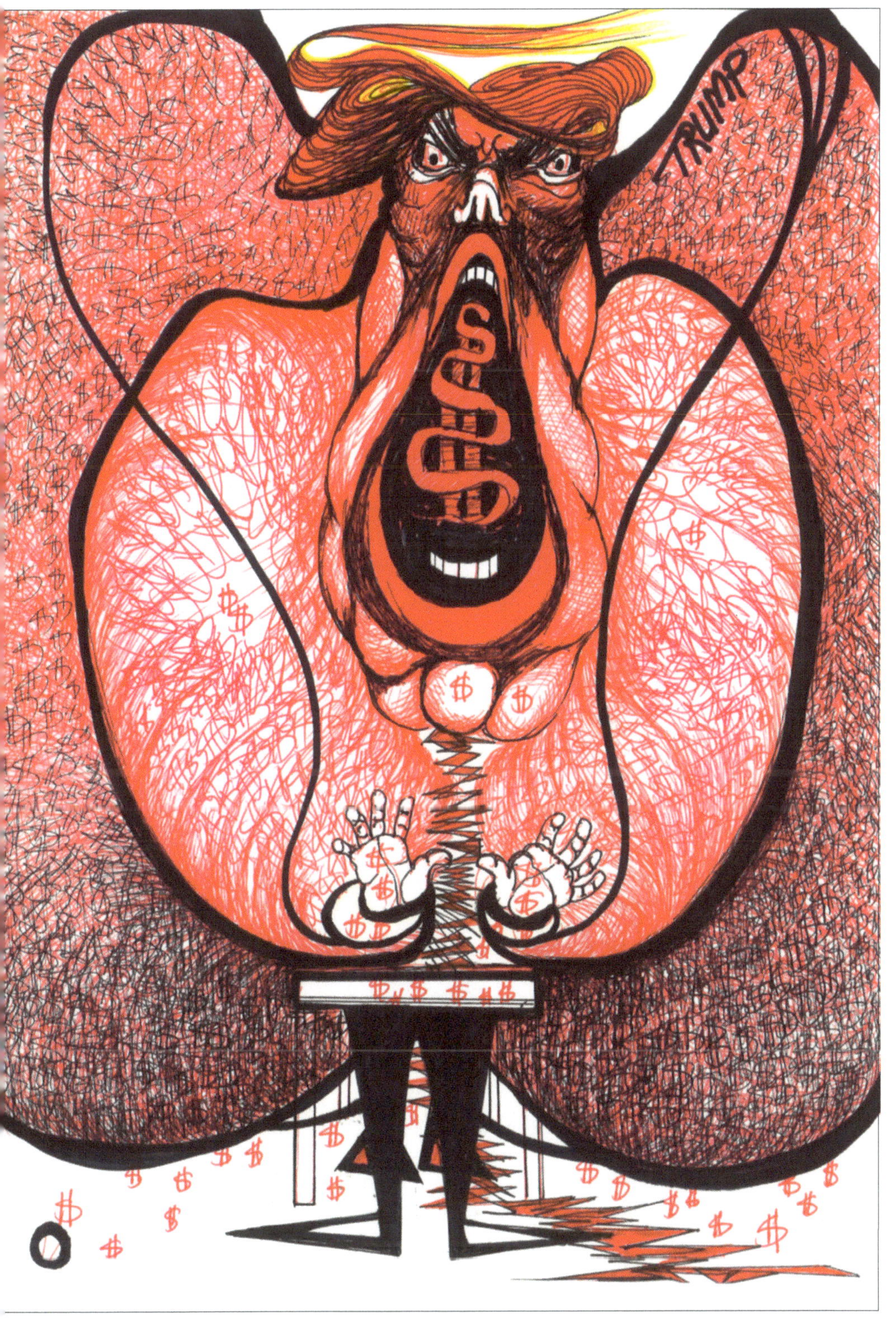
TRUMP

This drawing was inspired by the book,"Bag Man" written by Rachel
Maddow which described the corruption of Spiro Agnew, Nixon's vice
president, who literally bagged cash from the White House and is
reminiscent of Trump's advisors—children and son-in-law—who were
bagging millions from their connections to the foreign countries.

Ivanka Trump and Jared Kushner
made millions in Washington, but at what cost?

NBC News, Politics and Policy

Wealth without Work

One of the "Seven Social Sins" from a Sermon given by Frederick Lewis
Donaldson in Westminster Abbey,
London, on March 20, 1925.

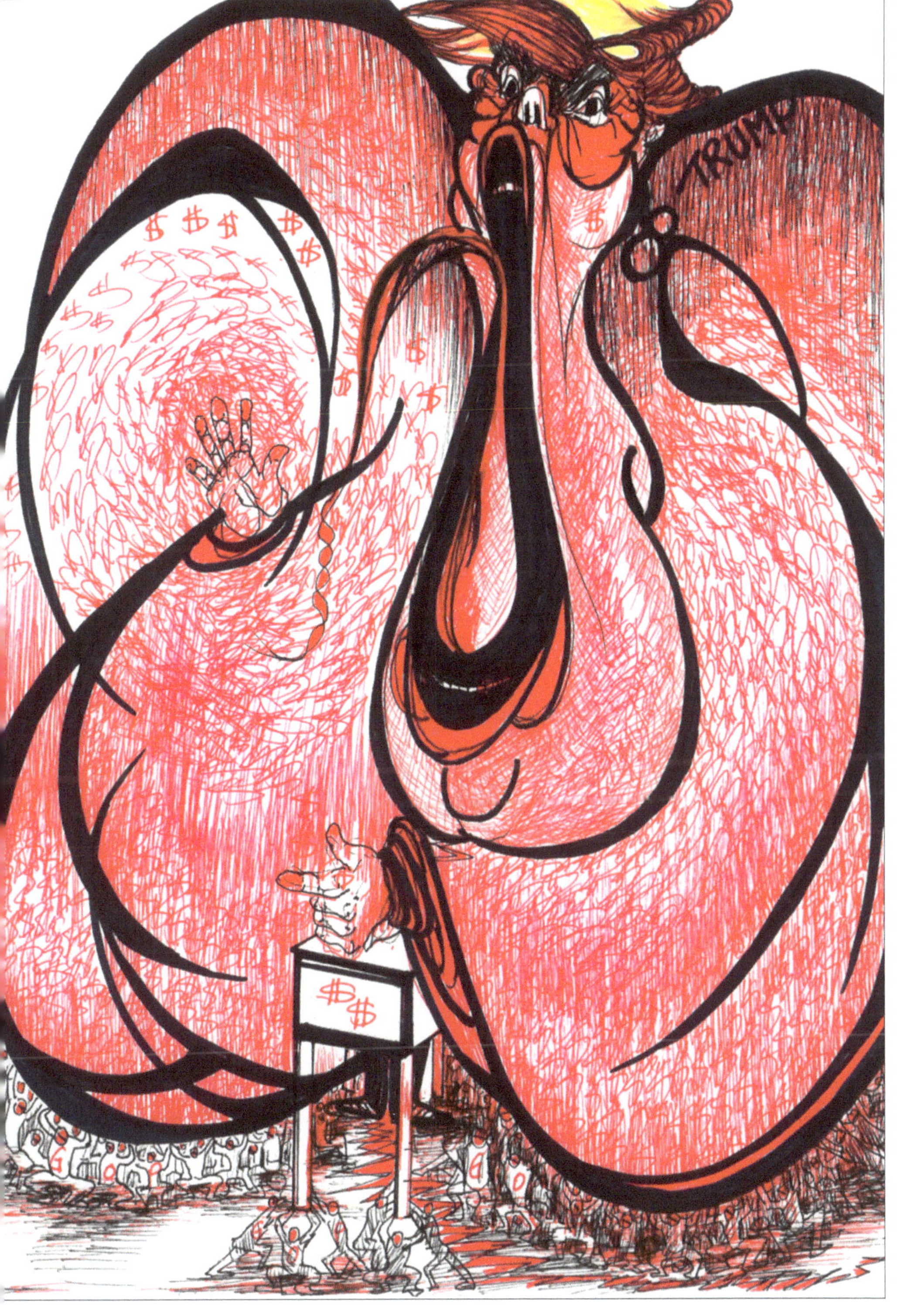

TRUMP

Acknowledgements

It is a privilege to draw.

Special thanks to my late husband, Kurt Hanselmann, for his unconditional love and support for me and for my art, as well as his unwavering influences that opened my awareness and re-enforced my desire to stand up for social injustices against humanity.

The motive of these drawings was not meant to be political; rather, it was an expression! I remember when I showed the first two drawings to my son, Nik, and my niece, Joancy. Both of them laughed hard and suggested that I submit them to The New Yorker—what an encouragement!

Since then, I kept my drawing momentum going and completed a large body of more than 100 drawings that I was proud of. I showed those drawings to an amazing friend who specializes in modern and contemporary art, Elaine. She encouraged me to find a venue to share the drawings with the public. But I still felt uncomfortable sharing the drawings on social media. I sought professional advice from my friend Mario, who has published comics books.

One day I brought the drawings to campus during his class recess so he and his students would have the chance to go over them with me. One of the students suggested that I put the drawings on Instagram, one drawing per day, so I would generate a group of followers. All these suggestions motivated me to put these works in book form.

During the 2023 Verge Annual Open Studio weekend, I showed these drawings to some of my artist friends, Linda and Carlaina, and both agreed that I should publish them. My thanks to all the most trusted audience. I did not include your last names within this acknowledgement, as I don't want to get you in trouble concerning these works, should they turn into unwanted political divisiveness. Special thanks to Jenifer Novak for her amazing expertise in helping to bring out "A Visual Diary" to light.

Brenda Louie, Fair Oaks, California

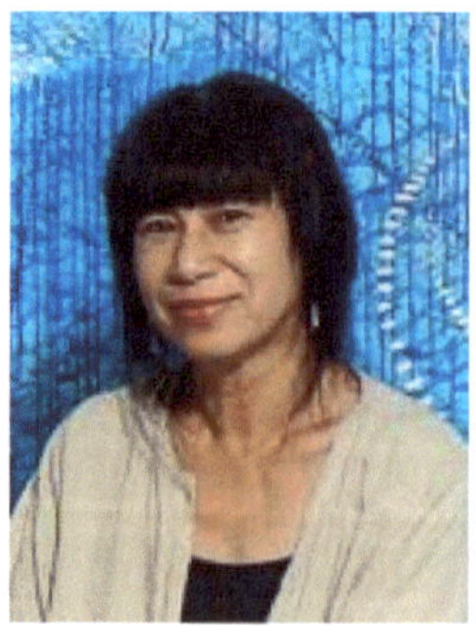

About the Artist

China-born American artist Brenda Louie's work demonstrates the uniqueness of different cultural experiences and explores experiential similarities as an approach toward developing a new visual language. This new form of language will be not just an amalgamation but will underscore the strength and contrast of its origins.

Louie is a California-based multidisciplinary visual artist whose work has been exhibited in regional, national, and international museums and galleries since the late 1980s, including the Monterey Museum of Art, Oceanside Museum of Art, Crocker Museum of Art in Sacramento, Nelson Art Gallery at the University of California Davis, Institute for East Asian Studies Gallery at the University of California Berkeley, Art Department Gallery at the State College at Trenton in New Jersey, and Jack Olson Gallery at Northern Illinois University in DeKalb, Illinois, as well as Zhejiang Art Museum in Hangzhou, and Art and Design Gallery in Ningbo University, Ningbo, P.R. China.

Louie earned her Master of Arts degree in painting and drawing from California State University Sacramento in 1991, and Master of Fine Arts from Stanford University in visual arts in 1993. She received her art training from esteemed contemporary artists such as Oliver Lee Jackson, Joan Moment, David Hannah, the late Nathan Oliveira, and the late Frank Lobdell. While at Stanford, she met leading artists like John Cage, Mel Chin, Ann Hamilton, Robert Storr, and Lorna Simpson; these interactions helped shape her creativity in thinking and developing her art. In addition, Louie studied Eastern philosophy under an internationally acclaimed scholar, Dr. Philip J. Ivanhoe, and Chinese art history with noted art historian Dr. Richard Vinograd during her graduate studies at Stanford University. Louie was the recipient of the Gorden Hampton Fellowship, the Robert Mondavi Fellowship, and the San Francisco Foundation's Edwin A. and Adalaine B. Cadogan Scholarship, as well as numerous awards and honors from Sacramento Metropolitan Arts Commission.

Her work is housed in private and public collections in the United States, China, and the Middle East, notably the Crocker Museum of Art in Sacramento, Wickland Oil Company in California, University of California Davis, China Academy of Arts in Hangzhou, Opera House in the City of Hangzhou, Zhejiang Art Museum in Hangzhou, and Ningbo University in Zhejiang, P. R. China. She has taught at Stanford University, University of California Davis as well as San Francisco Art Institute. Louie was a faculty member of the art department at California State University in Sacramento, where she taught studio art from 1996–2019. Louie served as visiting artist at Normal University in Hangzhou in 2002, Ningbo University in 2008, Ningbo, Zhejiang, P.R. China, and Northern Illinois University in DeKalb, Illinois, in 2012.

For your information, please visit:
https://www.brendalouie.com
http://www.instagram.com/brenda.louie.art

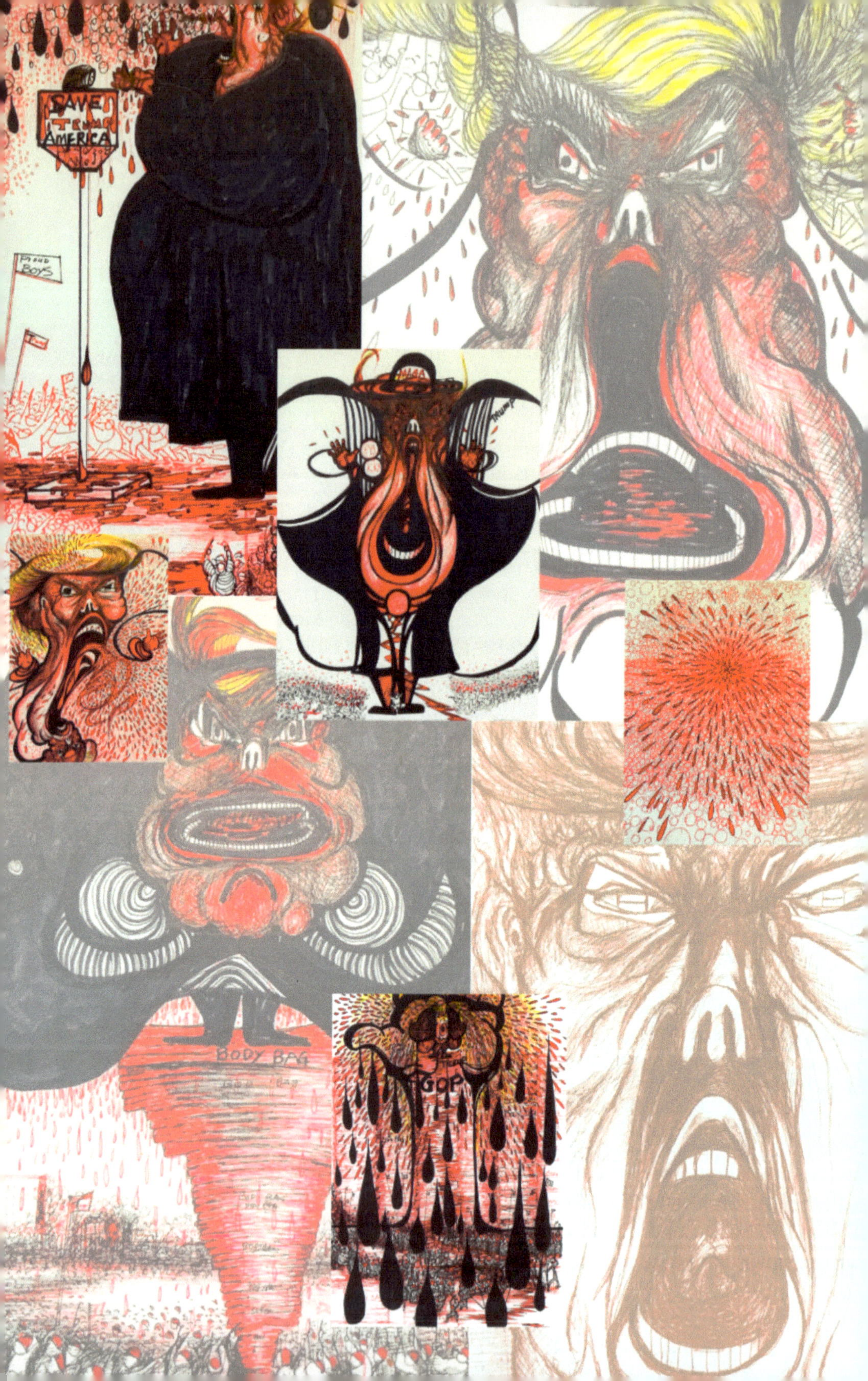
SAVE
TEXAS
AMERICA
PROUD
BOYS
MAGA
TRUMP
BODY BAG
GOP

www.ingramcontent.com/pod-product-compliance
Lightning Source LLC
Chambersburg PA
CBHW041224050726

47599CB00001B/69